Messner Books by Robert Fischer

GETTING YOUR ACT TOGETHER
How to Become a Child Actor or Actress

HOT DOG!

Getting Your Act Together

by

Robert Fischer

illustrated with photographs

JULIAN MESSNER NEW YORK

JULIAN MESSNER and colophon are trademarks of
Simon & Schuster, registered in the U.S.
Patent and Trademark Office.
Manufactured in the United States of America

Design by Virginia M. Soulé

Library of Congress Cataloging in Publication Data

Fischer, Robert, 1947-
    Getting your act together.

    Includes index.
    Summary: Discusses ways that children can build a
part-time or full-time career in acting including tips
on auditioning, getting an agent, and what to expect on
the job.
    1. Acting—Vocational guidance—Juvenile literature.
2. Children as actors—Juvenile literature. [1. Acting—
Vocational guidance. 2. Vocational guidance.
3. Children as actors]   I. Title.
PN2055.F5 1982   792'.02373   82-60638
ISBN 0-671-34041-7

For
Christopher Murray . . .
a good friend and a good actor

Acknowledgments

I would like to thank the following people for their help and support in seeing this project through to completion: my brother Danny and his wife Linda; my editor, Robert Hernandez; typists Therese Ray and Susan Redman; photographer Robert Maib; and my good friends Midge Poynter, Frank Montalbano, Ginger McKay, Don Stolar, and Lonnie Halouska.

Contents

Getting Your Act Together

Do you like to play make-believe? This young actor is being transformed with makeup. (Robert Fischer)

Introduction

Do you want to become an actor or actress? Do you like to imitate the way people move and talk? Do you often pretend that you're someone else? Do you feel like you're on top of the world when you're in front of an audience?

Do you have a good memory? Are you willing to work hard and take instructions? Are you always on time for appointments? When someone gives you a job, do you finish the task?

Do you have a lot of patience? Are you willing to work to stay healthy and fit? Do you get along well with other people?

If you can answer "Yes" to all of these questions, you are ready to try for an acting career. But you may wonder what some of these questions have to do with becoming an actor. Perhaps you believe (as many people do) that being an actor is easy. It's just a matter of standing in front of a camera or on a stage and performing. It certainly looks effortless when a skilled actor is doing the job.

Acting is hard work. Becoming an actor now, when you're young, doesn't make it easier. Acting for you may also mean giving up a lot of baseball games, school dances, and afternoons of roller skating. It's letting go of your daydreams and finding out the hard truth about the entertainment field.

The purpose of this book is to help you to discover what being in show business is all about. You may decide that acting is not for you after you finish reading about it. At least you'll understand and appreciate what the young people you see on television and in the movies have endured to get where they are.

On the other hand, you may finish reading the last chapter and still want to become an actor. You'll then be ready to take the first step toward reaching your goal.

Breaking Into Show Business

This chapter could be called, "How Not to Break Into Show Business," because much that you will learn disproves some of the myths about how actors and actresses get their first big breaks.

One myth is that you must have a relative or a close friend who is already a big star. Look at Tatum O'Neal, for instance. Wasn't she selected for the movie "Paper Moon" just because her father, Ryan O'Neal, was so well known?

There's no doubt that having a famous father didn't do Tatum any harm, but it was her great talent that actually got her into films and kept her there. The fact that she won an Oscar at the age of nine proves that.

Ryan O'Neal acted with his daughter, Tatum, in the movie "Paper Moon."
(Museum of Modern Art/Film Stills Archive)

Six-year-old Sara Stimson's mom worked as a secretary for the Veteran's Administration. There wasn't any show business connection there, but Sara played the leading role in the remake of "Little Miss Marker." Although she had no acting experience at the time of the auditions, she was chosen from more than 5,000 other girls for the part.

Sara Stimson had no previous acting experience when she starred with Walter Matthau in the 1980 remake of "Little Miss Marker." (Museum of Modern Art/Film Stills Archive)

Justin Henry got the role of Billy in "Kramer vs. Kramer" in the same way. His father works as a manager for the J.C. Penney Company. Justin had to compete with 700 other boys for the part. He also had no acting experience, yet he was nominated for an Oscar when he was only eight years old.

Dustin Hoffman played a divorced father who discovered the joys of fatherhood with son Justin Henry in "Kramer vs. Kramer." (Museum of Modern Art/Film Stills Archive)

Perhaps you've seen Ricky Schroder play T.J. in "The Champ." His dad works for the telephone company, but Ricky was lucky enough to have an older sister who began modeling for magazine advertisements when she was three years old. Ricky followed in her footsteps when he was only three months old. His later success in TV commercials, especially one for Kodak which also featured a sheepdog, gave him some good experience in front of a camera. His face was already familiar to many directors and producers, but he still had to compete with 5,000 other boys for his first big film role.

Ricky Schroder made his screen debut as T.J. in the 1979 remake of "The Champ." (Museum of Modern Art/Film Stills Archive)

19

Gary Coleman, who is Arnold in the television series *Diff'rent Strokes,* started his career at the age of six by modeling in fashion shows. He was soon doing commercials for McDonald's, Hallmark Cards, and Crackerjacks. Eventually, a television producer saw him and asked him to do the part of Stymie in a television remake of *The Li'l Rascals.* That show didn't work out, but *Diff'rent Strokes* certainly did.

Gary has also done guest appearances on such popular TV shows as *Buck Rogers,* and he has his own company, which produces TV specials. What do his parents do? His father works as a pharmaceutical supply inspector and his mother used to be a nurse.

Kristy McNichol is a very skilled and versatile actress who would have been successful no matter what sorts of jobs her parents held. She was fortunate to have a mother who worked as a secretary in a talent agency and who had appeared as an extra in a few movies. Kristy's mother did help seven-year-old Kristy get a job in a television commercial, but it was Kristy's talent which enabled her to go on to make fifty more commercials and to win an Emmy Award for her role as Buddy Lawrence in the television series *Family.* Since then she's starred in television and feature films and has performed a singing and dancing act with her brother Jimmy.

Another show business myth is that you have to live in or near Hollywood in order to get a job as an actor. It's true that Kristy McNichol, Willie Aames (*Eight is Enough*), and Quinn Cummings (*Family* and "The Goodbye Girl") are from the Los

Kristy McNichol (seated, center) talks to her fellow campers in ''Little Darlings.'' (Museum of Modern Art/Film Stills Archive)

Angeles area. On the other hand, Ricky Schroder lived in New York City (and now in Connecticut), Justin Henry in Rye, New York, and Sara Stimson in Helotes, Texas. Gary Coleman was living in Zion, Illinois, when he first started working.

If you still aren't convinced that where you live makes

little or no difference, consider the following facts before you try to talk your folks into pulling up stakes and moving to Hollywood:

- Although most commercials are shot in Los Angeles and New York City, many are also shot in Chicago, San Francisco, Dallas, and other towns and cities.

- Many film and television production facilities are located on the West Coast, but the corporate head-quarters for the film companies and television networks are in New York City. The process of *casting* (selecting actors and actresses) is done on both coasts.

- Many films are made on location throughout the United States and even the world. Sometimes local residents are hired for the smaller roles.

- Many daytime soap operas film in New York City.

You can see that where you live isn't going to make or break you in show business. The important factor is that you're right for the role and available to do the part.

Have you heard that acting school is a "must" if you want a chance to audition for a movie? The truth is just the opposite. Beginners are usually expected to have a certain amount of natural acting ability, but no one expects them to be polished performers. If you've taken some singing and dancing classes, you might have an advantage over someone who hasn't, but even that training isn't a necessity.

Some talent agents may suggest that you enroll for a few sessions with a good acting coach. However, the way most youngsters learn about acting is by doing it on the job. The more jobs you get, the more skilled and at ease you'll become.

There is one useful ability that some acting classes can teach you. If you have enough money and time, attend a school that shows you the techniques for auditioning and for improving your chances of getting jobs. The instructors will give you hints on what to say and do, and, more importantly, what *not* to say and do. Such knowledge will enable you to appear much more natural and at ease when you're face-to-face with a casting director.

If you're over twelve, you can get some free acting experience by appearing in school plays or in films that are made by students taking college or university film courses. If you're in high school, there might be some drama classes that you can join. Any such experience can be very helpful, but it's not necessary to have any experience. The biggest advantage to be gained from any drama class is that you'll probably be more used to being in front of an audience. The less nervous you are, the more likely you will be to impress the director.

WARNING! There are a number of excellent acting schools that accept both children and adults, but there are also some that are more interested in only getting your money.

Some of these schools will advertise that they promise to get you a top-ranked agent or even a job after you graduate. These are empty promises. No one can make such guarantees.

If you decide to attend an acting school (especially one that advertises a lot), check to see if there have been any complaints filed against it. Call your local Better Business Bureau, or the Consumer Fraud Division or your local district attorney's office. If there have been no complaints, go one step further and ask the school's director to show you his license and to name some of his well-known graduates. Find out exactly what you'll learn in the classes and just how big those classes are. Check to see how long he's been in business in your area.

If all of the answers satisfy you and your parents, go ahead and sign up. If you're not happy with what you find out, don't hesitate to turn around and walk away.

You may have seen advertisements that say, "Here's your chance to make it big in the movies. Enter our contest and you may win the chance of your lifetime to fly to Hollywood and star in a scene with your favorite television or film personality."

Is this opportunity really the chance of a lifetime? Is it possible to break into show business by winning a contest? A few people would say yes. Fourteen-year-old Ed Finnerman of Springfield, Massachusetts, and thirteen-year-old Tim Hussey of San Lorenzo, California, won a D.C. Comics drawing contest and a chance to go to Calgary, Canada, to appear in the movie "Superman."

Winning a contest seems like an easy and surefire way to

start on the road to stardom. However, such contests, even if they are honestly run, usually lead to nothing more than an appearance in a mob scene or in a small "walk-on," or non-speaking, part.

But don't extras and walk-ons have a good chance to eventually get bigger and better parts? Everyone has heard stories of an unknown being discovered by a director because his or her face stood out in a crowd.

The reality is that almost all extras remain extras. Unless you're a member of the Screen Extras Guild (SEG), you won't even get that kind of job. The SEG doesn't encourage newcomers because there aren't enough jobs for those people already in the union. The members of this union are likely to work only about two or three days a week. The chances that any of them will be discovered and move up to stardom are remote.

If you become a member of the SEG, you'll have several advantages over nonmembers when it comes to getting work. One big advantage is that being an SEG member will automatically qualify you for membership in the Screen Actors Guild (SAG) after one year has passed. There's no doubt that SAG members have much better chances of finding jobs. Even if a director or producer just interviews you for a job as an extra, he must pay you for that time. Interviews are rare, however. Most extras are chosen from the pictures that they send in with their applications.

If you're interested in appearing in an occasional film, but really don't want to make a career out of show business, then being an extra might be just the right thing for you. Such work can be a lot of fun, and you'll learn many interesting things and meet exciting people. Check the white pages of your telephone book or call information for the number of the Screen Extras Guild office in your area. If you live near Hollywood, you can also call Central Casting.

Some young people break into movies, television, or commercials by working as models for live shows or advertisements. Others work as actors in professional stage productions or by doing "voice overs" for cartoons or commercials. In a voice over, the audience will hear you speak but won't see you. These jobs can be as hard to get as a regular acting job, but the experience will be a big plus in finding more work as an actor. Your membership in the unions or guilds that cover this kind of work will also qualify you for a SAG card when one year has passed.

You may be able to get your first acting job by attending open casting sessions. In open casting, a film or television company advertises for people to come and try out for a certain role in a certain production. The ad tells what type of character is needed, and anyone who thinks he or she might have the qualifications for the part can try out for it. Sometimes an experienced actor will have the edge over a newcomer in an open casting session. Just as often, however, you may have the "new" face or personality that will attract a director's eye.

The following ad appeared in one of the trade or business newspapers when Paramount Pictures was advertising for people to attend an open casting session for the role of Engleberg in the movie "The Bad News Bears." Trade papers are read by most people in the entertainment field and by those who are just trying to get their first job. They print news about what's happening in the business.

Some ads might print "SAG film" in the copy. Those words mean that if you get the part, you'll have to be paid a

This is an actual ad that appeared in *Daily Variety* for casting the part of Engleberg in "The Bad News Bears."

certain minimum amount of money. It doesn't mean that you won't get the part if you're not a SAG member. The producer can hire a nonmember if that person is the best one for the role. If you go to such a casting session and get the part, you are then eligible to become a SAG member. In some cases, you're required to become a member.

Always pay attention to what is written in an ad for an open casting session. There's no point in going to one if you're not the type they're looking for. Also, some open castings for university or nonunion films are for roles for which the actors will get little or no money. You should be aware of that possibility, but remember that if you get the part, you'll gain experience. If you're just getting a start, that's worth more than any amount of money.

There's something else to be aware of when you see an open casting ad. Some of them are invitations to get you to enroll in some sort of acting class. If you don't recognize the name of the production company, call the Producers Guild to see if the production is legitimate.

If you're serious about getting into acting, consider subscribing to one or more of the trade publications, such as *Variety* or the *Hollywood Reporter*. News about the upcoming open casting sessions can be found in them, plus information about many other opportunities for young actors and actresses, such as new plays and films that are being planned.

The trade publications also print lists of casting agents. You could send some pictures of yourself plus a short letter describing your experience and other qualifications to as many casting agents as you can.

If you want to appear in commercials, you could send your pictures and the letter directly to the big advertising agencies, plus any casting agents who work in commercials. Some of these may be listed in the telephone book. You can also call and ask casting people at the ad agencies how they go about finding the people who appear in their commercials.

Another way to find work is to list yourself in the *Academy Players Directory*. After you do all of these things, get a telephone answering service or machine if you can afford it. It is important not to miss any calls if there is no one at your home.

Does all of this sound like a lot of work? There is a way to make things easier on yourself. You don't have to wear yourself out making the rounds of casting directors, open casting sessions, advertising agencies. Instead of sending out endless letters and pictures and sitting by the telephone waiting for a call, you can get someone else to do all that for you. That someone is called an agent. An agent gets paid with a percentage of your wages. A good agent is worth every cent that he or she makes.

2 Finding the Right Agent

Since agents make a living by taking 10 percent of your pay, it's easy to understand their reasons for working hard to get you good jobs. How do they find those jobs? First, they sign agreements or contracts with actors and actresses whom they believe have the talent and other qualifications that are necessary to succeed in show business. The people with whom they have signed contracts form a group called the agent's "stable."

Agents are always talking to producers, directors, and anyone else who might need someone to fill a role in a production. They also read the trade papers and the newspapers and follow up on any leads they can find that might lead to a part for one of their clients.

When a picture is being cast, agents "screen" their stables to find just the right people for the roles that are being auditioned.

An agent is actually a middleman who matches the actor with the job. If you can find an agent who will agree to work for you, your chances of getting jobs will increase immediately. You'll save yourself a lot of time waiting in line and hoping for telephone calls that may never come.

How do you find a good, honest agent? You have to do some research to find out which agencies handle young people and what type of entertainment they specialize in. If you live near New York City or Los Angeles, one way to find the right agent is to look through the children's section of the *Academy Players Directory*. Find the names of the young people you've seen on television and in the movies, then see who their agents are. You'll get a pretty good idea of which agents are successful in finding work for their clients. There is also a complete list of agents in the back of the directory.

There are also lists of agents in the trade papers. Some of these agents are very well known and have good reputations. Others are honest and hard working but may be just starting their careers. You probably won't recognize their names, but they might be more eager to sign a contract with you than someone who is more established.

There are a few agents who are dishonest. Some of them actually just try to get students for their acting schools. You can weed these people out by checking with the Artists Managers Guild, 9255 Sunset Boulevard, Suite 930, Los Angeles, California 90069. The telephone number is (213) 274-0628. Write or ask whether or not the agent you're considering has a contract with the Screen Actors Guild. If the answer is "No," forget that agent. He or she won't be able to get you any work.

Some local agents are listed in the yellow pages of your telephone book under theatrical agents. You can also call the Screen Actors Guild office nearest you. There are offices in nineteen cities, and they all have lists of agents they'll be glad to give you.

Choose five or six agents that handle young people, and send each of them a brief, typed letter. Have someone help you if necessary. Simply state that you're looking for an agent. Then describe yourself, giving your weight, height, color of eyes and hair, and any distinguishing characteristics. If you've had any professional acting experience, be sure to mention that fact. Make sure there are no errors in the letter, and include your return address and phone number. Conclude the letter by stating that you'll call for an appointment within a few days.

Include some clear pictures of yourself. If you want them returned, enclose a self-addressed, stamped envelope that's big enough to hold them. Some agents prefer professional photographs, but others will accept good snapshots that show your face well.

Occasionally, if your letter and photo impress an agent, he or she will call you. Don't count on such a call, however. Plan on telephoning him or her about a week after you send the letter. When you ask for an interview, you might be turned down, but don't take the rejection too hard. It's possible that that particular agent would like to handle you, but he or she may have all of the clients he or she can take care of at that time.

Don't ask the agent why he or she refused to interview

you. Just try the next one on your list. If two or more agents offer to see you, don't hesitate to see all of them. Just be sure to let each one know that you're considering other people. A good agent will know that having interviews with different people is the only way you can find someone that's just right for you.

What can you do if you reach the bottom of your list and you haven't succeeded in getting even one interview? Perhaps you could take a closer look at the letter you've been sending out. Does it say what you really want it to say about you? Maybe the pictures don't do you justice. Getting a different photographer may solve that problem.

It might be better if you wait another six months before

A good full-face photograph is needed for an actor's composite. This is Kristy McNichol. (Paramount Pictures Corporation)

33

sending out a new letter and pictures to the same agents that you've already contacted. In the meantime, you can try to get interviews with some new agents.

If you keep on being turned down for interviews, take a closer look at your career goal. Maybe it's time to think about getting into another phase of show business at a later date, such as camera work, set building, or costume design. Perhaps you could choose a future profession in which there's not so much competition and use your acting ability in amateur theater productions. You do have to face the fact that even the most skilled professional actors often aren't able to make a living in films or on the stage. They have to combine their skills so they can pay the rent and buy food.

Nevertheless, you should remember one important thing. The people who make it to the top in any field are the ones who don't give up easily. If you want to become an actor more than anything else in the world, especially now while you're young, by all means, keep trying. If you have enough talent, your persistence may eventually wear down even the toughest agent's resistance. He or she knows that being able to stick to something in spite of difficulties is one of the most important traits that an actor or actress can have.

Let's suppose that an agent calls you to schedule an interview. Here are some ideas on how to make the most of the opportunity.

First of all, dress neatly, but don't overdress. Don't chew gum. Bring a book to read so you won't get impatient if you have to wait. Having something to keep your mind busy will also keep you from getting too nervous.

Don't be upset if the agent can't see you at the exact time of your appointment. Perhaps he's on the telephone getting jobs for his clients. If you become one of those clients, that's what you'd want him to be doing.

During the interview, the agent will be looking at the following qualities.

Appearance. You don't have to be a raving beauty or stunningly handsome to get work as an actress or actor. Nevertheless, the agent will be sizing you up to see if you fall into any of the types of roles that are currently being cast. He'll also be thinking about his other clients to decide whether or not he has too many of one certain type. If he has five "Huckleberry Finn" types already, and you're also one, the agent may have to turn you down. He may also have too many "girl next door" types, and while you'd be perfect for such a role, he probably won't take you.

It's possible that your looks are so unique or unusual that there would be very few roles that are right for you. Again, you'll be rejected through no fault of your own.

If you're a member of a certain ethnic group (black, Mexican, Oriental, American Indian, etc.), you may have an advantage if there are pictures coming up which will need certain types. However, your heredity may work against you if there aren't many parts being cast with minorities.

Intelligence. The agent will ask how you're doing in

school. If your grades are low, the school officials probably won't give you permission to work, so there's no point in continuing the interview. Low grades are also an indication that you may not be willing to put forth much of an effort. This trait will be a disadvantage in show business. Acting requires a lot of concentration and hard work. Every agent takes that into consideration.

The agent will also want to know how well you read. Poor readers have a hard time understanding scripts and memorizing lines.

Personality. The agent wants to know whether you're outgoing, shy, full of mischief, fun loving, aggressive, or passive. He'll be judging these traits from the answers you give to various questions and from the way you behave during the interview. If you fuss with your hair, fiddle with objects on the desk, or can't sit still, the agent will know that some of your movement is caused by nervousness, but too much squirming may work against you.

Attention span. The agent will try to see how long you can pay attention to one subject. Can you hold up your end of the conversation over an extended period of time? Are you a good listener? These skills are important for an actor to have.

Acting skills. The agent may give you a page of script to read so that he can see how well you dramatize the lines. He may give you some hints about a certain character so you'll have a better idea of how he wants the lines to sound. As you respond to his hints, he'll be able to tell how well you understand and follow directions.

You may also be asked to "improvise," that is, to pretend

that you're a certain person in a certain situation without a script to follow. The agent will want to see how well you use your imagination to make the character come to life before his eyes. Improvisation is a good way for an agent to tell how much natural acting ability you have.

Special skills. The agent may ask you about any special skills besides acting that you may have. Tell him everything you can think of that may be helpful in your future show business career. Can you sing, dance, or play a musical instrument? Can you handle a sailboat or ride a horse? Are you a good baseball player or swimmer?

When the agent stands and offers to shake your hand and thanks you for coming in to see him, the interview is over. At this point, don't linger. He's found out all he wants to know. If you take up more of his time, he may become annoyed. More often than not, he won't make up his mind on the spot, but will want some more time to think about whether or not to offer you a contract. He may say, "I'll be calling you to let you know my decision." If you haven't heard from him within a week, call him back.

Be prepared for him to say that he's not going to handle you as a client. Even if he was impressed with you as a person and as an actor, he may already have as many clients as he can take care of. Ask him to recommend another agent to you. He may or may not do so, but your question will let him know that you don't get discouraged easily. That will be a big point in your favor.

A few words about rejection are appropriate here. Every

actor and actress, no matter how talented, has had to face many rejections. If you want to make your living in show business, you'll have to learn one important rule: it really doesn't make any difference how many people say "No" to you. Just keep looking until you find the people who say "Yes."

So just take a deep breath and go on to the next agent on your list. The day may come when you find the right one, and he'll offer you a contract. Before you and your parents sign it, have it read by a theatrical attorney. If he or she says it's fair and legal, you've found yourself an agent. Go ahead and sign it. Then go out with your friends and family to celebrate.

Your Agent and You

The first thing your agent will ask you to do is to go to a professional photographer for some pictures. He or she may recommend someone who specializes in theatrical photography. Such a photographer may cost more, but he or she will give you better pictures for your money.

Order two or three large black-and-white photographs, or "glossies," that show your face at its best angle. You'll also need several other pictures—full-face shots and full-figure shots of you in action. You could be playing racquetball, or dancing, or catching a baseball. You could also include a couple of shots that show you in costume. The agent can help you pick the photos that he or she thinks will get the best attention from a casting director.

Your agent will help you put together a "composite," which is a three-hole-punched sheet of dull-finished paper that has your full-face picture on the front plus your name. On the

An arrangement of full-figure and character shots should appear on the back of your composite.

back, arrange some smaller shots of yourself, and list your real or stage name, birthdate, hair color, weight, height, and your agent's name and telephone number.

Your agent may suggest that you think of a stage name that will improve your chances of getting a job. A young girl named Frances Gumm changed her name to Judy Garland. With her talent, beauty, and personality, Judy might have made it to the top in spite of her real name. There's no doubt, however, that her new name helped her to get her foot in the door of the entertainment business.

Many famous people use stage names. Could John Wayne have built up such a "tough guy" image if he had used his real name, Marian Morrison? How about Sparky Marcus, who played Ogilvie on *The Bad News Bears* TV series? His real name is Marcus Gordon Issoglio.

Creating a good composite costs anywhere from seventy-five to several hundred dollars, depending on your photographer's prices. Get the best pictures that you can afford. Remember that they'll be sitting side-by-side with those of many other young people who are after the same job that you are.

Your agent will send your picture and composite out to the various casting agents and directors. He or she may also have you listed in the *Academy Players Directory* in the children's category. You'll have to pay a few dollars for this listing, but it's worth the expense. The directory is a two-volume book that is published three times a year. Casting people use it constantly when they are trying to fill a certain role. There are five listings on a page, each of which contains

Judy Garland is frightened by the wicked witch in "The Wizard of Oz."
(Museum of Modern Art/Film Stills Archive)

one or two pictures of an actor or actress along with his or her name and the agent's name and telephone number.

Much of an agent's work is done on the telephone. Sometimes a casting director calls and asks for a client by name. At other times he'll just ask for a certain type of actor to fill a certain part. Before your agent sends you to an interview with any casting director, he'll check to see that the producers of the movie have signed a contract with the Screen Actors Guild. The guild protects your rights as an actor or actress. You won't be sent to a nonunion producer for an interview.

The following is a typical telephone call from a director to an agent.

"Hi," says the director. "Listen, I need the following: Twin girls, ten to twelve, with freckles for a gum commercial. A red-headed boy with braces, fourteen to sixteen, five-foot-eight to five-foot-ten for an acne product, but he needs to have a clear complexion. One boy, blond, blue-eyed, athletic for camping equipment. Four kids, two boys, two girls that all look alike for a family with dark hair, brown eyes for a car company."

The agent will take notes, then get to work to find just the right boys and girls for the director's "shopping list." Maybe you'll be one of them.

The agent doesn't just sit and wait for people to call. He or she also reads the trade papers to see who's casting. Smart agents stay in close touch with producers, directors, and casting people outside of office hours, too. They talk to people at parties and take them to lunch so they can be the first to know about the roles that become available for their clients.

When your agent is able to match you to a part that looks just right for you, he or she will set up an interview with the casting people. Your agent will let you know where to go and when to be there and maybe give you some hints on what to wear and how to behave.

At this point, your agent has done all that he or she can. It's going to be up to you to impress the casting director with your ability, your self-confidence, and your energy. No agent in the world can get you a job unless you live up to your part of the bargain.

When you get your first part, your agent will negotiate the contract and the price for you. An agent will make sure you're not underpaid, but he or she won't ask for too high of a price either. Overpricing yourself can lose you a lot of future jobs.

Your agent will help you to make the most of any acting jobs you get. He or she might place an ad in the trade papers to let other producers know when and where you're appearing. Some producers may come to see your performance on a stage or watch for the film in which you appear. If you impress them, they may be calling your agent to ask if you can appear in one of their productions.

Your agent may run an ad about you in the trade papers even before you get a job. This ad will act as an introduction to the people who read it. The more they see your name and picture, the more likely they will be to remember you when the right part comes up.

After you've had several jobs, your agent will help you to prepare a resume. A resume lists information about you and the acting jobs that you've had. If a difficult role has to be filled, a producer will often want to use someone with experience. Your resume might help you land one of these jobs.

Your agent will help you to decide which career move to take next. If you're doing nonspeaking parts in commercials, he or she will know when you're ready for speaking parts. Your agent will advise you about whether to take a certain movie role or whether to go after a television series. He or she will help to guide your career, prevent you from overworking, and see that you get more money and better parts as you gain more experience while pursuing your acting career.

There's nothing better than to have a good working relationship with your agent. There's every reason to develop such a relationship. After all, you're both working toward the same goal—to get you acting jobs.

3 | The Audition

Let's suppose that your agent has scheduled you for an audition or a job interview. Now, suddenly, you wish you could forget about the whole thing. Your nerves are jangled, and your stomach is full of butterflies.

A little nervous tension is good. It keeps you alert and enables you to perform at your very best. Many top stars, who have appeared in front of audiences for years, still have a lot of nervous tension before they walk onto a stage or in front of a camera.

Too much nervous tension can turn you into a stuttering, stumbling wreck, however. You're going to have to deal with getting rid of all of the unnecessary worries and fears that surround you. Your agent can help calm you down by telling you about the part you're auditioning for and by explaining what an audition is like.

Dress neatly for your interview or audition but don't overdress. Your best school clothes will probably be just right. SAG regulations don't allow producers to require you to audition in costume, but if you know that the part you're trying out for is in a western, it might be a good idea for you to wear blue jeans and a plaid shirt. *Don't* arrive in a cowboy hat, boots, chaps, and spurs, and twirling a lariat. The producer wants to see you, not a costume. Overdressing might even lose you the part if the competition is close.

Plan to arrive at your interview fifteen minutes to a half-hour early. If you get there any sooner, you'll have too long to wait and might build up a case of nerves. Don't arrive late.

Sign in with the receptionist as soon as you get to the office or studio. You may be given some pages of dialogue, so spend any extra time you have reading them. There may be other youngsters reading their lines, too. Perhaps they'll be saying them out loud to themselves or to their parents. Don't be embarrassed to do the same. The practice will be good for you. You're not required to memorize any script for an audition, but becoming familiar with it will help you to relax.

Remember to read not only the lines you'll supposedly be asked to say but also all the others. Some directors will ask you to switch parts.

One advantage of being familiar with your lines is that you'll be able to glance up often during your audition. The director will be able to see your face instead of the top of your head.

Use common sense and courtesy while you're cooling

your heels in the waiting room. Don't make a pest of yourself by continually asking the receptionist when you're going to be called. The director wants to stick as closely to the schedule as possible, so he'll be doing the best he can to get to you. Also, if you're a SAG member, if you're kept waiting for more than an hour after your appointed time, the director or producer will have to pay you for your time.

If the other people in the waiting room seem friendly and are interested in talking to you, carry on a quiet conversation. Always remember that there might be someone who is rehearsing his lines, so keep your voice down. Don't ever quiz anyone for information about the role for which you're auditioning. Such behavior is considered unprofessional, and even if you're not a professional actor yet, you want people to think you are.

Rowdiness, of course, is out of place in any waiting room. Anyone who forgets this rule may be asked to leave without being given a chance to audition.

When your name is called, go straight into the director's office, leaving any books or homework in the waiting room. Don't be encumbered by any extra baggage. Carry only your picture and your composite and any papers or material that the receptionist might have given you.

When you walk into the office, you may see other people besides the casting director. Perhaps the producer will be there. If you're auditioning for a commercial, there might be a representative from the product's advertising firm. There might be another actor or actress there also.

You may be asked to read the script that the receptionist

gave you, or you may be asked to read some other script. The director may give you some ideas about the part you're doing, or he may ask you to read the lines in several different ways. He may ask to see how well you "mime" (act out some situation without saying anything), or he may give you a situation and ask you to make up some lines for it.

In an audition, there's often someone else to exchange dialogue with you. Many offices have videotape machines, so the director can put your audition on videotape and study it later.

If you go to an interview or an audition for a commercial, you may be asked to sample the product. If you bite into a candy bar, or taste some cold cereal, pretend that you like it even if you don't. *Never* make faces or make fun of the product. That's a sure way to lose a job before you even have a chance to get it.

The most important rule to follow during an audition is to pay attention to what the director says and follow closely any instructions he or she may give to you. At the same time, be yourself, so the director can see what you're really like.

If you "flub" a line, don't be afraid to ask if you can try it again. If you do get a second chance, be careful not to make the same mistake again.

When the interview is over, the director will thank you and show you to the door. Thank him and leave promptly. Don't ask him whether or not you got the part. He probably won't know. Your agent will call him later to find out the results of your audition.

If you are invited back to do another reading, you can be

sure that the director was impressed with you. During this second audition, you may be asked to exchange some lines of dialogue with one of the stars of the upcoming show, and there will probably be some more people there to look you over. If you're called back for a third time, there's a double reason for celebration. You're one step closer to getting the part. At this point, SAG rules say that you have to be paid for your time.

There are very few people who get every part they audition for. You'll be no exception. After a third audition, your hopes will be high, but you can still lose the part. Being turned down hurts, but you have to forget that hurt and keep trying for other parts. Persistence does pay off if you have talent. Look upon each audition not as something to dread, but as a wonderful opportunity. Keep telling yourself that you wouldn't have been able to get that audition if your agent or someone else didn't think you have a lot going for you.

Depend on your agent to schedule your interviews or auditions. But depend on yourself to handle the auditions without letting your nerves get the best of you. If you start to shake, just take a deep breath and give it your all. You'll soon find that you actually enjoy those auditions.

One day you'll get a telephone call from your agent. "You got the part!" he'll say. "Congratulations! Your call is for Monday morning at seven o'clock."

That's one telephone call you'll never forget.

4 Acting is a Job

"Early to bed and early to rise . . . ." That old expression may have been first stated by someone working in the entertainment field. When you finally start your professional career, you'll find that your days will be so full that you won't object to crawling into bed early.

Now that you have a job lined up, the first thing you're going to have to do is to apply for a work permit, which will give you legal permission to be employed. These permits are required by state and federal laws which were designed to protect young people. Before such laws were passed, children often worked ten to twelve hours a day. They were paid very low wages and were exposed to hazardous conditions. These conditions appeared not only in the entertainment field, but in factories and on farms.

Your agent will be able to tell you exactly how to get your work permit and give you an idea of the working conditions that are legal in your state.

California has some of the strictest child labor laws in the United States. They set the maximum amount of time that a youngster can legally be on a shooting set and the amount of time he or she can be in front of the camera. For older children, who can work up to eight hours total, the laws require that the time be divided with an hour for lunch plus three hours of schooling during the eight-hour period. Every young person must have a parent or a legal guardian with them while they're working. Your parent and your studio teacher will see to it that you're not forced to do any dangerous stunts and that all of the other child labor laws are followed.

During the time that your permit is being processed, the director will give you a script which you'll have to study at home. You have to become thoroughly familiar with not only your own lines, but also the lines of everyone else. Otherwise, you won't know what your "cues" are. A cue is a signal for an actor to speak a line or do some sort of action.

Studying the script also gives you a feeling for the type of person you're supposed to be in the movie or play. Will you be very active? Are you going to have to cry, laugh, or be angry? Are you going to have to climb a fence or tackle a fleeing bank robber? Or are you going to have to be a timid, sickly type of person?

Along with the script, you may get a "call sheet," which

lists the times that everyone in the cast will have to appear on the set. The call sheet will also list the scenes that are to be shot on a particular day. Your job will be to memorize the lines for those scenes and become familiar with your cues.

You may have to be on the set at seven or seven-thirty in the morning. You *must* be on time, because in filming a movie or a commercial, every minute that passes means that more money must be spent. Every director and producer is very aware that he has only a certain amount of money to spend. You need to be aware of this also.

If you need a costume for your role, you will be fitted by the wardrobe mistress. For most shows, you'll be told ahead of time what to wear. When you arrive at the scene of the filming, or "shooting," you'll go to the area set up for the makeup and hairdressing people. Your hair will be brushed or styled before each day's shooting so it will look the same throughout the movie.

You'll start your day's work with school or with filming, depending on the day's shooting schedule. If the filming comes first, the producer or director might have you run through your lines with the dialogue coach. While the lights are being positioned, your stand-in will take your place on the set. In the meantime, you may be asked to rehearse the scene with the other actors or actresses.

When everyone is ready, an assistant calls, "Quiet!" A buzzer will sound once as a warning that shooting is about to start. The director then calls "Sound," and the tape recorder is

Jodie Foster played a gangster's girlfriend in "Bugsy Malone." Her makeup and hair had to be carefully styled to look the part. (Museum of Modern Art/Film Stills Archive)

turned on. A few seconds later, the soundman says, "Speed," to let the director know that the tape recorder is ready to record. The director calls out, "Camera!" When the cameraman is ready to start filming, he replies, "Rolling."

An assistant will be in front of the camera with a clapstick marker that shows the number of the shot and which "take" is being filmed. A take is one filming of a certain shot. There may be many takes before the director is satisfied that the shot has been filmed just the way he wants it.

The assistant will call out the information about the shot and the take that is being filmed. Then he'll say "Marker," and hit the clapsticks together. This information is recorded by both the camera and the tape recorder.

The assistant and the marker will be moved out of camera range, and the director will say, "Action." It's now up to you and the other actors to come up with a successful take. Everyone else on the set will be quiet while the cameras and recorder are rolling.

When the take is over, the director calls, "Cut," and the soundman sounds the buzzer twice. The makeup people might touch up your makeup, and the director might make some suggestions as to how to improve the next take.

The lights will have to be reset whenever there are any shot changes. During these breaks in shooting, you may be sent to the studio school. Sometimes you'll be the only one in the classroom. There will often be other youngsters from different grades and of varying ages. The teacher will instruct each of you according to what your regular school has been teaching you. He or she doesn't want you to fall behind in your regular classes. If the film is being shot during the school year, you'll be told to bring your books and homework with you to the set.

Around noon, you'll have a one-hour lunch break. If you eat in the studio commissary, you might see some stars. There may be actors and actresses dressed in anything from space outfits to Indian costumes. After lunch, you can read or do whatever you want. Just be careful not to make any noise outside of the sound stages that have a flashing red light. That light means that there's filming going on inside.

You probably won't work past three-thirty. At that time, you'll hang up your costume and wash off your makeup and get your call sheet for the next day.

By the time you go home and have supper, you might have an hour or two to play or to watch TV, but you'll probably have to spend some time doing your homework or memorizing your lines for the next day's shooting. Then it's into bed by eight or nine, because you'll have to be up in time to get back to the studio for your early morning call.

Does it sound like a hectic sort of life? It is. Of course, some days are easier than others. If you're not scheduled for any scenes, you'll just go to the studio school in the morning and maybe go home after lunch.

During the summer you won't have to go to school, but you'll still have to work if you're cast in a film. While your friends are going swimming, skateboarding, and playing games, you'll be doing endless takes or trying to fill the empty time between scenes.

When you're not working, you'll return to your regular schedule of school and homework and play with your friends. Be aware, however, that those friends may not treat you the same as they used to. Some of them might be a little envious of you. Others will think that you have changed, although you won't think you have. These problems may grow as you become more successful in your career until you find that you have more friends in the studio than you do in your neighborhood.

Todd Bridges of *Diff'rent Strokes* said, "I'm just a regular person."

Just keep being yourself, though, and your friends will soon accept you again. They'll find that actors and actresses are really no different than anyone else. Instead of earning money by having a paper route or by babysitting, they earn their money by appearing in a film or a commercial.

You'll also gain a new group of friends among the people on the cast and crew. Sharing each other's successes and failures and problems will bring all of you very close. Sometimes you may even feel as if you've acquired a second family.

5 Being an Actor

Acting is not only hard physical work. It can be hard emotional work as well. Sometimes you'll be given a role which will seem easy because the character is very much like you. In other words, you can just be yourself. Eventually, however, you may be asked to play a character who isn't like you at all. Perhaps you'll have to be the class bully or the snooty rich girl. These are people you wouldn't like at all if you met them in everyday life. Nevertheless, such a role is challenging as well as difficult.

As an actor, you have to use your mind and your body to communicate ideas, feelings, and attitudes to an audience. The more you know about people and the better your physical health, the more effective you'll be in your career. Swimming, bicycling, or playing a team sport will help you to keep healthy. You can also eat good, sensible food and get plenty of rest so you're always full of energy and ready to do your best. Bathe daily and wash your face several times a day to keep your complexion clear. Pay attention to your teeth so your smile will be attractive. Dirty or bitten fingernails may lose you a job in a commercial in which you'll have to display a product.

Classes in fencing, karate, or dancing will help you to move gracefully and to control your body movements. Yoga can help you to learn breath control, and singing will help you to gain voice control. Playing a musical instrument can give you a feeling for rhythm and timing. All of these things can make you a better actor, because they'll help you to coordinate your body movements.

Actors are usually very curious people. They want to know how other people feel, live, and think. Get into the habit of observing everyone around you. Look at how they move, and listen to the way they speak and to the things they say. Watch the actors on your favorite television shows. Pay special attention to their eyes, their facial expressions, and the way they use their hands to show emotion. Even when they're not saying anything, they're reacting to what's going on around them, just as people do in real life.

Even the most experienced actors and actresses sometimes have trouble getting a characterization or a scene to work just right. You'll have the same trouble occasionally. Your director's job is to help you over these rough spots. The director will know not only how a certain role should be played, but also how to get you to play it that way. The director might demonstrate how to say the lines and how to move. Maybe the director will just give you some ideas that will help you to use your imagination to "get into your character's head."

Most directors who work with young people have a lot of patience and an ability to communicate just what they want. Don't be afraid of your director. After all, you're both working toward the same goal, and he or she wants to help you get there.

One of the hardest things to do is to cry during a scene when you don't feel sad at all. The director may ask you to think about an unhappy moment in your life. If you think about it long and hard enough, the tears will come. During the making of "The Champ," Ricky Schroder had to cry a lot. Thinking about the death of his beloved grandmother brought the flood of tears that appeared on the screen.

Franco Zeffirelli directs Ricky Schroder and Jon Voight in a scene from "The Champ." (Museum of Modern Art/Film Stills Archive)

If many takes are required, you may become "cried out." At that time, no matter how hard you try to "think sad," the tears won't come. Don't worry. The makeup man will then be brought in to perform some film magic. A drop or two of glycerine makes a big wet tear on an actor's cheek.

If you're in a television series, you'll have to do the same role week after week. Even when you're doing a commercial, you may have to go through a dozen or so takes before you're through. Each time, you need to act as if it's the first time you've bitten into that hot dog or jumped rope in that certain brand of blue jeans. As an actor, your enthusiasm or lack of it will come through on the film. You must love what you're doing, or it would be best to think about getting into some other sort of career.

6 Movies, Television, and Commercials

Acting is acting, whether it's done on a stage, before a live audience, or in front of a camera with only the stage crew and the other actors and actresses present. The mechanics and techniques of acting vary, however, depending upon the circumstances. Acting in a movie is different from acting on a stage. Doing a television series is different from appearing in a commercial.

Acting in the movies has changed over the past sixty or so years. Young actors and actresses such as Shirley Temple and Jackie Coogan used to sign contracts with a particular studio. Whether or not they were appearing in a film at a particular time, they would draw a salary. As a result, when a movie came along which required a child star, the studio would use a young actor that it had under contract. One actor might play

Shirley Temple sings in this shot from the original 1936 version of "Little Miss Marker." (Museum of Modern Art/Film Stills Archive)

the villain in one picture, a crippled child in another, a brave hero in a third, and a shy "new kid on the block" in the next. These young people really had to stretch their acting abilities to do a wide range of different roles.

Today's studios don't put child actors under contract. Young people are chosen to fit a certain part and signed up to do that one picture. The role they play is likely to be very close to their own personality.

Ricky Schroder's optimistic personality and his love of life shone through when he played in "The Champ." He also had a close off-screen friendship with his co-star, Jon Voight. The combination was a winner.

When Jackie Cooper played the same role nearly fifty

John Voight cheers with Ricky Schroder in the 1979 remake of "The Champ." (Museum of Modern Art/Film Stills Archive)

years earlier, he had no off-screen rapport with his co-star, Wallace Beery. Jackie's acting talent made his performance a success, but it's likely that two such people wouldn't have been cast together in today's Hollywood.

To understand the big job facing a movie actor of any age, you have to understand how a movie is put together. It's not produced like a stage play, in which the actor starts at the beginning of the story and plays the role straight through to the end. A movie is made in bits and pieces, because filmmakers must cluster their shots around a certain location or set. They must finish all the shots that take place there at the same time,

Jackie Cooper sits on the shoulders of Wallace Beery in the original movie of ''The Champ.'' (Museum of Modern Art/Film Stills Archive)

whether or not those shots take place at the same time in the finished film. The set is then dismantled and another one built, or the cast and crew are moved to another location, where the shots are all done at once. Sometimes all the scenes in which a high-priced star appears will be shot together so that the production only uses the star's services for a few weeks instead of months. This shooting "out of sequence" is done to save time and money, but the process can be confusing to someone who's not used to it.

A good director can help you to understand what's happening and can give you ideas about exactly what's going on in the story so your performance can fit the plot and appear smooth in the finished film. Since the character you're playing may change a lot from the beginning of the film to the end, you're going to have to figure out just how he'd be behaving at that time in the story. Depend on your own feeling for the person you're portraying plus your director's guidance and you'll be all right.

Some movies, or parts of them, are still shot in studios. Many of them are shot on location, though, because today's audiences demand realism. Shooting on location means using a real downtown location to film a ghetto scene, or a real desert to film a story about a thirsty group of pioneers, or a real seaport to film a pirate story.

Filming at all these different places can mean some drastic changes in an actor's way of living for a few weeks. When you're on location, you'll sleep in hotels on unfamiliar beds and eat foods that may not be the type you're used to. Even with one of your parents with you, you may get homesick for the rest of your family and friends. You may wonder why it takes months to shoot a picture that lasts only two hours when it's finished. You'll have to learn to be patient. The director doesn't want to save time and money by hurrying through the various scenes. The scenes often have to be shot and reshot many times before the actors speak their lines and react to each other in the desired way. If each scene is successful, then the finished film has a chance of being a hit.

Often a scene has to be shot more than one way. First a master scene is filmed with all the actors in the scene. Then the proper close-ups or two-shots (two actors together) of the stars are filmed. The people in the scene have to repeat their lines and their actions again and again to make sure they have enough shots that blend into the scene before it and the one that will come after it. When all of the completed shots are edited together, with just the right shot emphasizing a line of dialogue or a reaction, the finished film will look like one continuous, uninterrupted series of scenes. As you view the film, it may be hard for even you to see where one shot leaves off and the new one begins. That's because of good editing and directing, and good acting, too.

Young actors and actresses today don't do nearly as many films as did the young stars of twenty or thirty years ago. As a result, many of them fill in the time between films by doing commercials and television shows. They quickly find out the differences between those types of jobs and the job of working in a movie.

Putting a television show together proceeds at a much

faster pace than the production of a film. Most one-hour TV shows are filmed in about seven days. Some time is allotted for retaking scenes, but not nearly as much as is in moviemaking. TV budgets are much tighter than movie budgets and deadlines are much shorter. When you're working in television you are much more aware of the clock, and that awareness often causes pressure to build up. You'll have to learn to deal with that pressure while concentrating on your role.

Television actors have to learn certain technical skills. One of the most important skills is knowing which camera to face. At times, there might be three TV cameras on at the same time. Your movements will have to be coordinated with each one of them. Don't be worried if you make some mistakes at first. Your director has worked with newcomers before, and he or she will teach you what you have to know. After you've learned, however, it's up to you to pay attention and get things right the first time, so no time will be wasted in retakes.

There are movies that are made just for television. Acting in them is like acting in a regular movie, except that everything moves along much faster. On the other hand, acting in a television series is quite a bit different from acting in a movie or a TV special. In a series, you'll be playing the same character week after week. If you're lucky, you may end up playing that character for two or three years. The character will have to grow and change as *you* grow and change. You'll be facing a great variety of television situations with that character, and you must have him or her keep the same basic personality throughout each situation and over a long period of time. You may be having problems in your personal life, but you can't allow those problems to interfere with the life of your television character.

What if you have to play a character that is quite different from the real you? Alison Arngrim plays the role of Nellie Oleson in *Little House on the Prairie.* Nellie is a nasty little girl who is not at all like Alison, yet every week Alison has to become Nellie for a certain number of hours.

Alison Arngrim (in bed) and Melissa Gilbert pose in this shot from the television series *Little House on the Prairie.* (NBC-TV)

Scott Baio, who plays Chachi in *Happy Days,* is perfect for playing that happy-go-lucky character. Scott has shown his ability to play other types of people, too. He was a young alcoholic hockey player in *The Boy Who Drank Too Much,* and he was a gangster in the movie "Bugsy Malone."

Scott Baio (center) starred as a gangster in the all-children cast of "Bugsy Malone." (Museum of Modern Art/Film Stills Archive)

Adam Rich appears as Nicholas in *Eight is Enough*. Nicholas is a lot like the real Adam in that he is athletic and a warm, friendly person. But Nicholas isn't nearly as smart as Adam, and he's also a couple of years younger than Adam is. Every week Adam has to use his acting ability to make Nicholas come to life.

There's one very good thing about appearing in a long-running television series. You'll have a continuous job from week to week and maybe from year to year. This is a type of job security which is seldom found in the movie world of today.

Acting in a commercial is different from acting in both movies and television. In a commercial, an entire story must be told in one minute or less. Portraying a character in that length of time is quite an accomplishment, especially when the real star of the story is a product, not a person.

Most young actors are chosen for a certain commercial because they so closely fit a look or character that the director has in mind. If the "parents" in the commercial have dark hair, their "children" will also have to have dark hair. The actors have to be the right age and height for the parts.

Acting ability is also very important, though. In a commercial, you have only a few seconds to impress the audience with how much fun a certain toy is, or how much fun it is to play a game. You'll have to express the delight you have in munching a candy bar, or how good a soup, or a certain type of sandwich spread is. The acting skills you learn by doing commercials will help you when you do movies and television shows. In fact, many young people and adults get their start in show business in this way.

Your ability to follow instructions well is a necessity in doing commercials. You must coordinate your speaking lines, your motions, your expressions, and your position on camera. You must do everything quickly. The few seconds that appear in the finished commercial often represent an entire day of hard work.

Commercials are an especially good way for young people to break into show business because so many children's products use children in their commercials.

Young people are also often used to promote products that only adults are interested in buying. Haven't you seen commercials for cars in which the mother, dad, kids, and family dog are all getting ready for a trip? How about the one for a detergent in which the mother tells her little boy or girl not to worry about a muddy jacket? *You* could be that boy or girl, couldn't you?

7 Building a Career

Getting your first job, moving from a small nonspeaking part in a commercial to a minor role in a movie, and improving your performance steadily are parts of the process of building your career.

A career doesn't grow automatically, like a tree. You'll have many choices to make, and sometimes the success or failure of your career might rest heavily on your decisions. At these crucial times, listen to the opinions of your agent and of your parents. Brooke Shields's mother and Tatum O'Neal's father felt that their children would do well in films that were geared toward adult audiences. On the other hand, Ricky Schroder's parents guided him toward the making of family films. In those cases, the decisions were right for their careers.

An actor or actress of any age must be prepared to handle

Brooke Shields starred in the 1978 movie "Pretty Baby." (Museum of Modern Art/Film Stills Archive)

the emotional stress of being in the entertainment field. If your career means a lot to you, you'll have to handle the "highs" and "lows" that go along with it. What if you thought your performance in a certain movie or TV show was great, but the critics' reviews don't reflect your feeling? There's nothing like a bad review to make an actor become depressed, because people who read such a review in the newspaper or hear it on the radio probably won't go to see the show.

The reviews in the trade papers can affect the way producers, directors, and other important show business people think about you. There's no doubt that a bad review can hurt your career, but you'll have to realize that it can't ruin your future. What happens next is largely up to you. Can you get over feeling depressed, learn something from what the critics said about your performance, and go on to do a better job the next time? If so, you've got a lot of what it takes to make it to the top. Eventually, you might gain enough self-confidence and good judgement to ignore some of the bad reviews. You'll know you did your best and that you did a good job in spite of what the critics said. Many times, you'll find that your audience will agree with you. The critics don't always agree, and they're wrong at times, too.

As your career progresses, it's possible that you'll be miscast in a show, or that the television series in which you're appearing will be cancelled. Being miscast means that your agent or the director put you into a part which isn't right for you. The cancellation of a TV show often doesn't have much to do with whether or not the actors and actresses are doing a good job. As long as you do your best in the show, you needn't blame yourself for any such failures. Such things are beyond your control.

Nevertheless, a cancellation of a show can still hurt deeply, especially if you've been on a long-running series. Most actors and actresses feel very close to their television "families," and they miss them more than they miss the money or the publicity. Gabriel Melgar played Raul on *Chico and the Man* for two years. When he was fourteen, the show was cancelled, and Gabriel found the news hard to take.

"Everybody told me it wasn't my fault, but inside I did feel it was my fault. It suddenly just went BOOM. That's all," he said.

Success can be almost as hard to handle as failure if you're not ready for it. What if your career takes off and you feel as if you've been left behind? Suddenly, you'll be surrounded by financial and investment counselors, accountants, agents to handle your personal appearances, tax and theatrical attorneys, people who run your fan club, and many others with the special skills it takes to keep a career going. You could end up feeling very closed in, and the loss of your private life can be frightening.

At this point, your best friends will be your parents and the rest of your family. Talk to them about how you feel and ask them for advice if you think that things are going too fast for you. With their help, you can fly as high as you want in your career, but your feet will still be firmly on the ground.

With a solid footing, you'll be able to deal with the successes of your career as well as the failures. Of course, one of the greatest successes you can have is to win a major show business award. Young Patty Duke won an Oscar for her portrayal of Helen Keller in a movie and an Emmy for the same role on TV. Her career received a great boost from those awards.

Just being nominated for such an award means a lot. Quinn Cummings was only ten years old when she was nominated for an Oscar for her performance in "The Goodbye Girl." The attention that she received helped her to land the role of Annie on the television series *Family*.

What's going to happen to your career as you advance from the cuteness of a seven- or eight-year-old to the awkwardness of a teenager and then into early adulthood? Some actors' careers weather the problems of growing up, but others don't. You have a good chance of making it if you're lucky enough to be in a successful television series during this time or if you have the persistence and the talent to get parts that correspond with the changes that take place in your life. Some young actors drop out for a few years, then come back as adult actors.

Ron Howard, who played Opie in *The Andy Griffith Show* and Henry Fonda's son in *The Smith Family*, got through the adolescent period in good shape. His role on *Happy Days* has been a consistent success, and he also directs films and is a producer for television.

Some young actors and actresses turn to other types of careers when they become adults. Others go to college and

Quinn Cummings consoles Marsha Mason in a scene from "The Good-bye Girl." (Museum of Modern Art/Film Stills Archive)

earn degrees in business and in other fields. Since their careers in show business teach them the value of hard work and patience, most of them are successful in their new professions.

Shirley Temple became the U.S. ambassador to Ghana. Jerry Mathers and Tony Dow played brothers in the television series *Leave it to Beaver*. After finishing their education, Jerry became a businessman and Tony entered the construction business. Recently, they became a team again in a play called *So Long, Stanley*. They found, as do many actors and actresses, that it's almost impossible to forget show business altogether.

Some of today's young actors and actresses are making plans for their adult years. Melissa Gilbert already has her own television production company called Half Pint Productions. Quinn Cummings wants to become a lawyer or a writer. Ricky Schroder is too young to make a final decision, but he wants to stay in show business if he continues to be a "good actor."

And what about you? One way to insure that you'll be successful in whatever you decide to do is to start saving the money that you get from your acting career. That money can pay for college and could later finance a successful business career, if that's what you want.

How much do young actors earn? The rate for a SAG member is now over $200 a day. That's the *least* you can earn for eight hours, although if you're hired for a full week, the daily rate could be less. As you become better known and are in more demand, you'll earn much more than the minimum pay.

If you work steadily in commercials, you can earn from $5,000 to $25,000 a year or more. A television series can earn you $150,000 a year. At least that's what Dana Plato of *Diff'rent Strokes* is reported to make. On that same series, Gary Coleman is reported to earn over half a million dollars a year! In the movies, a top young star can make that much for one film!

And that's just the beginning in some cases. You also earn money from "residuals," which are payments that are made to you when a TV show is rerun or played in a foreign country, from each time a commercial is shown on TV, and when a movie is sold to a television station. These residuals can eventually total the amount of money you were originally paid, but the payments are spread out over a long period of time. You not only get paid for the work you currently do, but also for the work that you did a year or several years ago.

There will be times when you're not working, but if you have been employed for a certain amount of time, you'll be able to collect unemployment insurance payments. Don't hesitate to take this money, because part of it is there because of money that is deducted from your paychecks. Your parents or your agent will help you to apply for it.

Does all this sound like a lot of money for doing something that you love to do? Perhaps it is, compared to what many people make, but remember that the actual money you receive isn't as much as you are paid. Your agent will get 10 percent of your pay. A manager could get 15 percent. You have to pay about one percent of your earnings to the SAG. Then come all of your expenses, such as lessons, clothing, travel, and secretarial fees. And don't forget income taxes.

The amount you'll end up with will certainly be more than you could be making with a paper route or running errands for the grocer. However, you probably won't be able to spend much of what you make. Your parents will probably see to it that most of it is put into a savings account or invested in some way so you'll have it when you're older. Todd Bridges gets a ten-dollar allowance a week. Quinn Cummings gets only one dollar a week. Just as everyone else does, they have to save up if they want to buy a new record album or a portable radio.

There have been some sad incidents in the past in which a young actor's family took his money and squandered it before he grew up. Jackie Coogan, for instance, found that his parents had spent every cent he made. As a result, a law was passed in California (unofficially called the Coogan law), which requires that at least 20 percent of a young actor's earnings must be placed in a trust fund until he or she turns eighteen.

What will happen to the other 80 percent of your money? Fortunately, most parents do save their children's pay for them. Nevertheless, to prevent what happened to Jackie Coogan, the SAG is trying to change the law so that all of a young actor's earnings (after expenses) can be placed into a trust. So far, the SAG has not changed the law. Each family has to deal with the money in their own way. In most families, there is no problem. The youngster receives his allowance, and his money is waiting for him when he becomes an adult. As you get older, you may participate in more of the money decisions that your family makes for you.

8 Your Parents and Your Career

Most parents want their children to grow up and work at satisfying careers. Most careers, however, are in the future. If you want to become a child actor or actress, that means working *now.* Unless your parents are supportive and can cope with some of the disadvantages of having a youngster in show business, there could be some problems facing you. A young actor's parents must do more than agree that you may have the talent and the ability to act. They must agree to participate in a lot of work and inconvenience, a lot of disappointment, and some failure. All of these factors affect not only you, but your entire family.

If you're lucky, your folks will agree that the advantages of being in show business outweigh the disadvantages. You will be able to earn your own money for your future education.

You can gain useful experience that may form a basis for a career as an adult actor. You'll be meeting and working with interesting and famous people. There may be many opportunities to travel and visit interesting places.

It is possible that your parents may have to invest some money to get you started in a career as a child actor. They will have to give you permission to work because they have to sign contracts for you. It will mean that one of them will have to be available to take you to job interviews. One adult guardian must also accompany you when you actually work.

If you pursue an acting career, it can change the whole focus of your family's attention. Your folks may have to take time away from your brothers and sisters. It can interrupt family life and vacations.

Your parents may not be willing to disrupt the kind of life they've built for themselves and their children. If both your parents work, it could be difficult for them to make the time to help you. If you're working, too, how will it affect them? What if you end up making more money than your parents? Most parents would be delighted, but some parents might feel displaced. Adam Rich's dad, a garage mechanic, was at first envious that Adam earned more than he did. After he got over feeling that way, he found that his son's acting career brought them closer together.

If you're on location, one of your parents or a guardian must accompany you. However, when Ricky Schroder shoots a film in Australia and Gary Coleman films in Los Angeles, it definitely causes a disruption in the lives of their families. Their dads can't travel as freely because they have their own jobs. If their mothers go with their youngsters, the family must be separated, sometimes for several weeks.

While some parents do push their unwilling children into show business, they are the exception instead of the rule. Most mothers and fathers worry about the effect that fame and earning a lot of money will have on their youngsters. They wonder if a child can grow up with a normal sense of values if he or she has too much money or if too many people give him or her too much attention. They hear stories about kids who break down under the pressure of show business.

Rocky Schroder's dad has some of these worries, but he believes that stardom won't affect his son badly. "Parents are the big thing whether a kid stays on the right track," he said. "If you have a good close family, you'll be okay."

Justin Henry's mother feels that same way. "I have not had one bad experience," she said, "that would lead me to believe the only alternative for my child is to grow up sick because he's in show business."

On a television program called *20/20*, reporter Geraldo Rivera did a special segment on child actors. He expected to find that they were pampered and spoiled, but instead he found that they were just normal, ordinary youngsters. The show's conclusion was that working as a child actor "could be damaging, but not necessarily."

The only ones who can really answer the question of whether or not being a child actor is worth the time, the pressure, and the effort are the child actors themselves. Sherry

Justin Henry's mother felt that acting in "Kramer vs. Kramer" was a good experience for her son. (Museum of Modern Art/Film Stills Archive)

Jackson, who appeared on the TV show *Make Room for Daddy*, said, "I traded my childhood for other things—glamor, excitement, adulation." Sherry felt that her childhood was "no childhood."

On the other hand, Angela Cartwright, who was on the same show, said, "I had a really happy childhood, though it was probably not like anyone else's."

Dick Van Patten, who plays Tom Bradford on *Eight is Enough*, started his acting career when he was seven years old. He thought his childhood was great. In fact, he said he had more fun than any kid he ever met. He's glad that two of his sons are also actors.

Ron Howard has never regretted becoming an actor. "At an early age, I learned to love something," he said.

It appears that whether or not acting is the right choice is up to the individual. If you really want to act more than anything else in the world, and if your family supports your decision, there's a good chance that you'll be happy in your career. You'll grow up knowing that you're doing what many youngsters only dream of doing. You will be able to turn your dreams into reality.

Speaking of reality, let's look at some hard facts. What are your chances of earning a good living as an actor? Of the 46,000 members of the Screen Actors Guild, 75 percent earn less than $2,500 a year from acting, 10 percent make between $7,500 and $10,000 yearly, and the rest earn more than $10,000. It's evident that the majority of professional film and TV actors barely make a living at their trade.

Of course, these statistics don't reflect the thousands of other actors who spend years trying to become SAG members and never make it.

If you look at these statistics and decide not to become an actor because of them, you've probably made the right decision. On the other hand, if you see them as a challenge, you may have what it takes.

If you really believe in your dream of becoming an actor, make the effort. Deal with becoming a working actor first. Becoming a star will take care of itself as you get more acting experience. Take the first step toward making your dream come true, then the second, and the third. No one is going to come looking for you while you're daydreaming in front of your television set. Take some positive action to reach your goal. Remember that you won't be a child forever.

Good luck!

Appendix

Selected Trade Publications

The rates quoted are recent, but may no longer be current. Canadian rates may be the same or higher. Foreign mailing is usually higher. Write to the publications for current rates.

Academy Players Directory. Academy of Motion Picture Arts and Sciences, 8949 Wilshire Boulevard, Beverly Hills, California 90211. Three issues published per year at $30 per issue.

Backstage. Back Stage Publications, Inc., 165 West 46th Street, New York, New York 10036. Published weekly (every Friday) at 75¢ per issue, $32 per year.

Casting Call. Mel Pogue Enterprises, 3365 Cahuenga Boulevard, Hollywood, California 90068. Published twice a month at 50¢ per issue, $13.95 for 26 issues, $22.95 for 52 issues.

Commercials Monthly. Goodwin & Harris, Business, Editorial, and Advertising Offices, 6515 Sunset Boulevard, Suite 401, Hollywood, California 90028. $10 per year, $1.25 (+75¢ postage) per issue.

Daily Variety. Daily Variety, Ltd., 1400 N. Cahuenga Boulevard, Hollywood, California 90028. Published daily at 40¢ per issue, $55 per year (includes special edition the last week in October).

The Hollywood Drama-Logue. Drama-Logue, P.O. Box 38771, Hollywood, California 90038. Published weekly at 75¢ per issue, $13 for 6 months, $19.50 per year.

The Hollywood Reporter. The Hollywood Reporter, Inc., P.O. Box 1431, 6715 Sunset Boulevard, Hollywood, California 90028. Published at 50¢ per issue, $63 per year (including special issues in February and the last week in November).

Ross Reports Television. Television Index, Inc., 150 Fifth Avenue, New York, New York 10011. Published monthly at $1.85 (+15¢ NY sales tax) per issue. To get single issues by mail, send check or money order for $2.20 (for non-New York addresses) or $2.35 for New York residents,

$9.50 for 6 months, $18.50 per year (+8% NY sales tax where applicable). All prices include postage.

T.G.I.F. Casting News.   T.G.I.F. Enterprises, P.O. Box 1683, Hollywood, California 90028. Published monthly at 60¢ per issue on the newsstands, 75¢ sample issue by mail, $10 per year.

Variety.   Variety, Inc., 154 West 46th Street, New York, New York 10036. Published weekly at $1 per issue, $45 per year.

Craft Unions

Check the white pages of your phone book for telephone numbers.

Screen Actors Guild (SAG) (motion pictures)
7750 Sunset Blvd., Los Angeles, California 90046
551 Fifth Ave., New York, New York 10017

The SAG maintains other offices in the following cities:

Atlanta, Georgia	Minneapolis, Minnesota
Boston, Massachusetts	Philadelphia, Pennsylvania
Chicago, Illinois	San Diego, California
Cleveland, Ohio	San Francisco, California
Coral Gables, Florida	Santa Fe, New Mexico
Dallas, Texas	Scottsdale, Arizona
Denver, Colorado	Seattle, Washington
Las Vegas, Nevada	Washington, D.C.
Lathrup Village, Michigan	

Screen Extras Guild (SEG) (motion pictures)
3629 Cahuenga Blvd., Los Angeles, California 90068
551 Fifth Ave., New York, New York 10017 (SAG affiliated)

The SEG maintains other offices in the following cities:
    Honolulu, Hawaii
    San Francisco, California

American Guild of Variety Artists (AGVA) [live performances but not legitimate theater, which is covered by Actors Equity Association (AEA)]
1540 Broadway, New York, New York 10036
6430 Sunset Blvd., Los Angeles, California 90028
    Write to the AGVA in New York for other regional offices.

American Federation of Television and Radio Artists (AFTRA)
1717 North Highland Ave., Hollywood, California 90028
1350 Avenue of the Americas, New York, New York 10019

The AFTRA maintains other offices in the following cities:

Albany, New York	New Orleans, Louisiana
Atlanta, Georgia	Omaha, Nebraska
Binghamton, New York	Philadelphia, Pennsylvania
Boston, Massachusetts	Pittsburgh, Pennsylvania
Buffalo, New York	Portland, Oregon
Chicago, Illinois	Racine, Wisconsin

Cincinnati, Ohio
Columbus, Ohio
Dallas, Texas
Denver, Colorado
East Peoria, Illinois
Fresno, California
Honolulu, Hawaii
Louisville, Kentucky
Miami, Florida
Minneapolis, Minnesota
Nashville, Tennessee

Rochester, New York
Sacramento, California
San Diego, California
San Francisco, California
Schenectady, New York
Seattle, Washington
South Bend, Indiana
Southfield, Michigan
St. Louis, Missouri
Stamford, Connecticut
Washington, D.C.

Index

About the Author

Robert Fischer was born in Hamden, Connecticut. Mr. Fischer was graduated from the University of Pennsylvania with a major in English literature and earned his Master of Fine Arts degree in Cinema from the University of Southern California. Mr. Fischer currently resides on both the East and West Coasts. His interests and hobbies include listening to music, reading, playing sports, and, of course, writing.